BRITANNICA BEGINNER BIOS

AMELIA EARHART

AVIATION PIONEER

DANIEL E. HARMON

Britannica
Educational Publishing
IN ASSOCIATION WITH
ROSEN
EDUCATIONAL SERVICES

Published in 2018 by Britannica Educational Publishing (a trademark of Encyclopædia Britannica, Inc.) in association with The Rosen Publishing Group, Inc.
29 East 21st Street, New York, NY 10010

Distributed exclusively by Rosen Publishing.
To see additional Britannica Educational Publishing titles, go to rosenpublishing.com.

First Edition

Britannica Educational Publishing
J.E. Luebering: Executive Director, Core Editorial
Mary Rose McCudden: Editor, Britannica Student Encyclopedia

Rosen Publishing
Kathy Kuhtz Campbell: Senior Editor
Nelson Sá: Art Director
Brian Garvey: Series Designer
Ellina Litmanovich: Book Layout
Cindy Reiman: Photography Manager
Bruce Donnola: Photo Researcher

Library of Congress Cataloging-in-Publication Data

Names: Harmon, Daniel E., author.
Title: Amelia Earhart: aviation pioneer / Daniel E. Harmon.
Description: New York: Britannica Educational Publishing, in Association with Rosen Educational Services, 2018. | Series: Britannica beginner bios | Includes bibliographical references and index. | Audience: Grades 1–4.
Identifiers: LCCN 2017015310| ISBN 9781680488067 (library bound: alk. paper | ISBN 9781680488050 (pbk.: alk. paper) | ISBN 9781538300206 (6 pack: alk. paper)
Subjects: LCSH: Earhart, Amelia, 1897–1937—Juvenile literature. | Air Pilots—United States—Biography—Juvenile literature. | Women air pilots—United States—Biography—Juvenile literature.
Classification: LCC TL540.E3 H375 2017 | DDC 629.13092 [B]—dc23
LC record available at https://lccn.loc.gov/2017015310

Manufactured in the United States of America

Photo credits: Cover, pp. 1, 6, 8, 20, 21, 23, 26 Bettmann/Getty Images; p. 4 Science & Society Picture Library/Getty Images; p. 9 Education Images/Universal Images Group/Getty Images; p. 10 National Archives, Washington, D.C.; p. 11 George Rinhart/Corbis Historical/Getty Images; p. 12 FPG/Archive Photos/Getty Images; p. 14 Underwood Archives/Archive Photos/Getty Images; p. 15 Collection 68/Alamy Stock Photo; p. 16 Everett Collection Historical/Alamy Stock Photo; p. 17 Aviation History Collection/Alamy Stock Photo; p. 18 Royal Air Force Museum/Hulton Archive/Getty Images; p. 22 Sueddeutsche Zeitung Photo/Alamy Stock Photo; p. 24 Corbis Historical/Getty Images; p. 25 Keystone/Hulton Archive/Getty Images.

CONTENTS

CHAPTER ONE

WHO WAS AMELIA EARHART?

Many women have contributed to progress in **AVIATION** during the past century. The most famous woman aviator was Amelia Earhart. She achieved many "firsts." Earhart was the first woman

Amelia Earhart poses with her Lockheed Electra—the airplane in which she crashed while attempting to fly around the world in 1937.

Vocabulary

AVIATION is the operation of aircraft that are heavier than air, including airplanes, helicopters, balloons, and spacecraft.

to fly alone, or solo, across the Atlantic Ocean and the first woman to fly solo from Hawaii to California. She navigated routes over land and sea that no woman had traveled before.

These were all amazing accomplishments for a young woman who grew up wondering what she might do with her life. Her family had little money. Airplanes in those years were rare—and dangerous. The facts that woman pilots were so uncommon and that she was so daring contributed to her enormous popularity.

Quick Fact

First Lady Eleanor Roosevelt was an admirer of Amelia Earhart's. She became a supporter and close friend.

Amelia Earhart is remembered for much more than the epic flights she made. Her life was important because she proved women can achieve what men can achieve. They can pilot airplanes across the country and across the oceans. If they have the courage, they even can set out to fly around the world.

The leather-jacketed aviator smiles from the cockpit of a small plane. Successful piloting requires years of training and experience.

CHAPTER TWO

CHILD OF A NEW CENTURY

Amelia Mary Earhart was born in Atchison, Kansas, on July 24, 1897. She was the first child of Edwin Stanton Earhart and Amy Otis Earhart. The family lived in Kansas City, Missouri, where Edwin worked as a lawyer. Amelia's parents were not good with money, and her father had a drinking problem. This caused stress and unhappiness within the Earhart family.

Amelia's sister, Muriel, was born two and a half years after Amelia. Soon after Muriel's birth, Amy and Edwin sent Amelia to stay with her grandparents in Atchison. For many years, Amelia spent the summers with her parents and the rest of the year with her grandparents. Amelia

A photograph shows three-year-old Amelia with her younger sister, Muriel.

enjoyed her time in Atchison. She spent many delightful hours playing in the barn and outdoors. She loved to experiment and to try new things.

Amelia first took to the air at the St. Louis World's Fair when she was seven years old. She was lifted high on a gigantic **FERRIS WHEEL**. She also was fascinated by the roller coaster at the fair, but her parents refused to let her ride it. When she got home, though, she and some other children put together their own makeshift coaster. She rode in a wooden crate down a track of boards from the roof of a tool shed to the ground. The landing was rough, but she was thrilled. Already, she felt the urge for fast motion and for soaring through the air.

Amelia was not the only person with this special spirit of adventure in the early twentieth century. The Wright brothers and other inventors were building and improving the first airplanes.

At age twelve, Amelia went to live with her parents again. They moved often as her father changed jobs. During her high-school

Amelia rode this Ferris wheel at the World's Fair in St. Louis, Missouri, when she was seven. It was her first adventure in the air.

Vocabulary

A **FERRIS WHEEL** is an amusement park ride consisting of a large wheel with seats around the rim. A motor turns the wheel to lift riders up and back down as the wheel spins.

The Wright brothers were among the earliest American aviators. Here, Orville Wright flies a biplane in a demonstration for the army.

years, she had few friends, but she did very well in her studies.

After high school, Earhart went to Pennsylvania to attend Ogontz, a college **PREPARATORY SCHOOL**. She was an excellent student. She played field hockey and other sports. A favorite hobby was her collection of article clippings about successful women who inspired her. She pasted these into a scrapbook.

Quick Fact

As a child, Amelia was a tomboy. Her father bought her and her sister balls, bats, and even a small rifle. They used it to shoot barn rats.

In 1917, the United States entered World War I. Earhart and her classmates became active in the war effort and formed the Ogontz Red Cross. While visiting her sister in Toronto, in Canada, Earhart was shocked at the sight of severely wounded soldiers who had returned home. She felt she should do something to help them. She decided to withdraw from Ogontz and move to Toronto. There, she became a nurse's aide at a military hospital.

Vocabulary

Students in a PREPARATORY SCHOOL take advanced classes to prepare them for college.

Although she posed for a graduation photograph at Ogontz school, Earhart actually left school before graduating. Instead, she went to work at a military hospital in Toronto during the war.

CHAPTER THREE

DOCTOR OR PILOT?

Much of Amelia Earhart's work in the hospital was depressing. Some of the wounded soldiers had lost arms or legs. Some were blind. She cared for the patients, feeding them and giving them medicine. She also mopped floors and helped keep the hospital clean.

Some of the soldiers were airplane pilots. She listened to their stories of flying with great excitement. One day, she and a friend went to an exhibition of **STUNT FLYING**. When a pilot flew very low over

From the earliest days of aviation, daredevils have thrilled crowds with airplane stunts.

the crowd, people scattered in fright—but not Earhart. She was thrilled.

While helping patients in the hospital, Earhart became dangerously ill. It took months for her to regain her strength. She spent that time thinking hard about her future. She was unsure what she wanted to do with her life. While she recovered, she took up several hobbies. She bought a banjo and took a course in auto mechanics.

Based on her nursing experience, she decided a medical career would suit her. She went to New York City and began taking courses at Columbia University to become a doctor. There were few women doctors in those days, but that did not worry Earhart. She was eager to demonstrate that women could accomplish what men could.

Vocabulary

STUNT FLYING is the performance in an airplane of daring feats such as rolls, loops, and steep dives.

For a brief time, Earhart lived in New York City. She attended Columbia University (*right*), thinking she might study to become a doctor.

Earhart moved to Los Angeles in the summer of 1920 to be with her parents, who had moved there. She intended to enroll in school in the autumn, but she soon lost interest in being a doctor. She became hooked on aviation.

One day, she and her father attended an air show. Earhart was dazzled by the planes zooming high above and swooping so low that spectators could see the pilots' faces. She told her father she wanted to learn to fly. He did not like the idea, but he hired a pilot to take her up for a joyride the next day. Rising from the ground, she

Neta Snook taught students at a flying school at a California airport. Although she was young, Neta was one of the country's best instructors.

was thrilled to see the Pacific Ocean in one direction and the famous Hollywood hills in the other.

She wanted to take flying lessons. Her family could not afford lessons, so Earhart found a job and earned the money herself. She asked Neta Snook to teach her. Snook was one of the country's rare female flight instructors. She was only twenty-four years old, but she had much flying experience. She was impressed by her new student. Earhart was a fast learner. She could handle an airplane better than most beginners.

Quick Fact

Neta Snook charged Earhart a dollar a minute for flying lessons. Snook also earned money by using her plane for advertisements and by giving aerial tours of Los Angeles and its surrounding area.

Earhart spent much of her time at the airfield. She learned all she could about how airplanes were constructed. She spent as much time in the air as she could afford. Unlike many fliers of the day, she was not interested in aerial stunts or joyrides. She considered flying an exciting sport. She simply loved being above the ground.

Earhart stands with a biplane she bought from an English woman. Earhart owned several planes during her short flying career.

CHAPTER FOUR

YOUNG WOMAN OF THE AIR

Earhart worked odd jobs and borrowed money to buy her first small airplane in 1921. It was painted yellow and nicknamed the Canary. The plane was very lightweight. This made it dangerous. She crash-landed more than once but never was injured seriously.

Earhart developed her flying skills quickly.

Earhart (*right*) poses with her friend and flight instructor, Neta Snook. Snook considered Earhart one of her most capable students.

She took advanced lessons and earned her pilot's license in 1923.

The following year, she gave up flying briefly. Her parents divorced, and she went with her mother to live in Boston, Massachusetts. Earhart returned to Columbia University but soon decided that she was done with school and moved back to Boston. There she worked as a social worker at a housing facility for immigrants.

In May 1927, Charles Lindbergh became the first person to fly nonstop across the Atlantic Ocean. It was an extraordinary feat. What would be even more fantastic, people thought, would be for a woman to cross the ocean in an airplane.

After crossing the Atlantic Ocean, Earhart, holding flowers, mechanic Louis Gordon (*next to her at left*), and pilot Wilmer Stultz (*next to her at right*) were treated like celebrities.

Vocabulary
In a **TICKER-TAPE PARADE**, spectators drop a flood of paper ribbons from rooftops and upper-floor windows down on the honored celebrity riding below.

A wealthy woman named Amy Guest owned a powerful plane and wanted a woman to be a passenger on a trip across the Atlantic. Earhart came to her attention because of her flying skills. She joined the team making the trip. Pilot Wilmer "Bill" Stultz and mechanic Louis "Slim" Gordon flew the plane and Earhart was a passenger.

They flew from Newfoundland to Great Britain in June 1928. It was the beginning of summer, but in the North Atlantic the weather was still cold. They flew through snow and ice. After twenty hours, they were running dangerously low on fuel. Finally, they saw the coast of Wales. They landed safely in a bay.

Earhart suddenly was famous. Thousands of people were eager to see her. She rode in a **TICKER-TAPE PARADE**

(*From top left to right*): Stultz, Earhart, and Gordon ride in a ticker-tape parade in New York City after returning from their 1928 flight across the Atlantic.

in New York City. She was paid to give speeches around the country.

Earhart was able to buy a larger airplane with the money she earned. She began flying long distances and setting records for distance, speed, and altitude, or height. A noted publisher, George Putnam, became her **PUBLICIST**. The two fell in love and were married in 1931.

Earhart made sensational history by flying solo across the Atlantic in May 1932. But making history was not her main purpose. She later wrote simply, "It was clear in my mind that I was undertaking the flight because I loved flying."

Soon after takeoff, her plane developed mechanical problems. It was buffeted by a storm. Its wings were covered with ice, causing it to spin toward the sea. Earhart barely regained control. Then a fuel line began to leak. But before the gas ran out, she made it to Ireland, landing in a small field.

George Putnam was a noted publisher. The couple are seen in Putnam's New York office after their marriage in 1931.

Vocabulary

A PUBLICIST is responsible for drawing attention to a celebrity or business.

Earhart was surrounded by well-wishers in Ireland after her solo flight across the Atlantic Ocean.

Now Earhart was more popular than ever. She wrote books and helped organize the Ninety-Nines, the world's first organization of women pilots. She started a clothing company. New airline companies asked her to help them get established. She visited the White House and became friends with First Lady Eleanor Roosevelt. The National Geographic Society presented her with its Gold Medal. She also became the first woman to earn the country's Distinguished Flying Cross.

Quick Fact

During her flight across the Atlantic in 1932, Earhart's only nourishment was one can of tomato juice.

CHAPTER FIVE

TRAGEDY IN THE SOUTH PACIFIC

Earhart made another historic flight in 1935, flying from Hawaii to California. The distance is longer than that from the United States to Europe. Earhart was the first person to fly the route successfully. That year Earhart also made record flights from Los Angeles to Mexico City

In Honolulu just before her historic Pacific flight in 1935, Earhart was given the traditional Hawaiian welcome with colorful garlands, called leis.

Vocabulary
The EQUATOR is the imaginary circle around the middle of Earth. It is about 25,000 miles (40,000 kilometers) around.

and from Mexico City to Newark, New Jersey.

Earhart soon decided that she would become the first woman to pilot an airplane around the world. Not only that—she would fly the longest route. This course would keep her near the **EQUATOR**.

In 1935, Earhart began an association with Purdue University in Indiana. The university established the Amelia Earhart Fund for Aeronautical Research. The fund

The Lockheed Electra in which Earhart tried her around-the-world flight was equipped with advanced devices for communication and navigation.

provided the $80,000 needed to buy a new airplane for her journey around the world. Her new twin-engine Lockheed Electra could carry enough gasoline to fly long distances between resting points. It had a powerful radio and other special equipment.

A photograph shows Earhart flying her plane over the Golden Gate Bridge in California, in her initial attempt to circle the globe.

The attempt to circle the globe took more than a year to plan. Her husband got permission for Earhart to fly in the airspace over different countries along her route. He arranged for gas, oil, and mechanics to be ready at the many airports and landing strips she would use. The project cost hundreds of thousands of dollars.

Earhart makes final preparations for her around-the-world flight in 1937. A little more than a month later, her plane was lost in the Pacific Ocean.

With a crew of three men, she took off from California on March 17, 1937. They planned to circle the globe flying westward. Sixteen hours later, they reached Hawaii. But when they tried to take off from there, the airplane swerved out of control and crashed on the runway. It was damaged badly. Earhart, uninjured but devastated emotionally, was determined to try again.

Two months later, the plane was repaired. This time, Earhart decided to fly eastward. She and Fred Noonan, her navigator, first flew from California to Florida. They took off from Miami on June 1. They flew to South America, then across the Atlantic to Africa. They crossed Africa, Arabia, India, and Southeast Asia to Australia, making about twenty-five stops.

On June 29 they touched down, exhausted, at Papua New Guinea. They were more than two-thirds of the way around the world. The next leg of the trip was crossing the vast Pacific Ocean. On July 2, they began a difficult flight toward a very small island in the mid-Pacific. The distance to Howland Island was some 2,500 miles (4,000 kilometers).

The Electra was never seen again. During the early morning of July 3, Earhart was in contact with a US Coast Guard ship. Its crew tried to guide her to the island, but

Quick Fact

Radio operators thousands of miles away claimed they heard weak radio distress messages believed to be sent by Earhart or her navigator. One message was allegedly picked up by Dana Randolph, a sixteen-year-old electronics buff in Wyoming.

they were not able to communicate with her. Earhart's last reports were garbled in static.

Ships and airplanes from several countries searched the ocean and nearby islands. No definite signs of Earhart or her airplane were found. Most historians believe the Electra ran out of gas, dropped into the sea, and sank.

Earhart's loss is mourned still, especially by those who press for equal opportunities for women. Throughout her life, Amelia Earhart was determined to prove women could accomplish what men could. She encouraged girls and young women to set high goals and to work hard to reach them.

TIMELINE

1897: Amelia Earhart is born on July 24 in Atchison, Kansas.

1916: After graduating from high school, Earhart enters Ogontz school.

1918: She serves as a nurse in Canada during World War I.

1919: Earhart enrolls in classes at Columbia University.

1920: She takes her first airplane ride.

1921: Earhart begins flying lessons and buys her first airplane.

1923: She earns her pilot's license.

1924: Earhart sells her airplane and moves to Massachusetts with her mother.

1926: She gets a job as a social worker in Boston.

1928: Traveling as a passenger, she becomes the first woman to fly across the Atlantic Ocean.

1931: Earhart marries George Putnam.

1932: Earhart flies solo across the Atlantic. She is awarded a gold medal by the National Geographic Society and is the first woman to earn the Distinguished Flying Cross.

Her first book, titled *The Fun of It*, is published.

1935: Earhart flies alone from Hawaii to California, a 2,400-mile (3,862-kilometer) flight over the Pacific Ocean.

1936: Earhart and her husband begin planning her around-the-world flight.

1937: Earhart and her navigator, Fred Noonan, take off from Oakland, California, on May 21 to begin their around-the-world flight.

Their Lockheed Electra is reported missing in the South Pacific on July 2.

1939: Amelia Earhart is declared dead on January 5.

GLOSSARY

ALTITUDE Height above the ground.

BUFFET To batter with wind or waves.

CONTRIBUTE To have a part in bringing about something.

DIVORCE To end marriage lawfully.

EPIC Unusually long, or great in size or scope.

EXHIBITION Public display of impressive skills or valuable objects.

EXTRAORDINARY Unusually impressive.

FACILITY Building or grounds used for a specific purpose.

IMMIGRANT A person who comes to a country to live there.

INSTRUCTOR Teacher.

MAKESHIFT Put together with an assortment of odd materials.

MECHANICS The work of building or repairing various machines, including automobiles and airplanes; also, the people who do that work.

NAVIGATE To plot and steer a precise course to a point of destination.

PUBLISHER One who prepares and produces books or printed works for sale.

RARE Very uncommon.

SENSATIONAL Very or unexpectedly excellent or great.

SPECTATOR Onlooker at a concert, sports contest, or other public event.

BOOKS

Barton, Jen. *What's Your Story, Amelia Earhart?* (Cub Reporter Meets Famous Americans). Minneapolis, MN: Lerner Publishing, 2016.

Bull, Angela. *Flying Ace: The Story of Amelia Earhart* (Eyewitness Readers). New York, NY: DK Publishing, Inc., 2000.

Kerby, Mona. *Amelia Earhart: Courage in the Sky* (Women in Our Time). New York, NY: Puffin Books, 2015.

Orr, Tamra B. *Amelia Earhart* (True Book). New York, NY: Children's Press, 2015.

Yomtov, Nelson. *Amelia Earhart Flies Across the Atlantic*. Minneapolis, MN: Bellwether Media, 2016.

WEBSITES

Because of the changing nature of internet links, Rosen Publishing has developed an online list of websites related to the subject of this book. This site is updated regularly. Please use this link to access the list:

http://www.rosenlinks.com/BBB/Earhart

INDEX